Unlocking the Unspoken

A 10-Week Self-Care Journal
to Unlock Faith and Hope

Copyright ©2025 Dr. Esmeralda Delgadillo

ISBN: 978-1-942923-92-3 (paperback)

Our Written Lives | San Antonio, Texas
www.OurWrittenLives.com

Scriptures from the English Standard Version (ESV) of the Bible.
Images are licensed for commercial use through Canva and Freepix.
Fonts licensed for commercial use.

This journal belongs to:

_____

_____

_____

To the Writer of New Truths,

Welcome my name is Dr. Esmeralda Delgadillo, and I'm a licensed professional counselor—but more than that, I'm someone who understands the courage it takes to begin healing. Whether you're holding silent grief, anxious thoughts, emotional fatigue, or hidden hope, this journal is for you.

I created this space to help you Unlock the Unspeakable: the thoughts you haven't said out loud, the truths you're just beginning to realize, and the healing you've been waiting to step into.

I invite you to begin speaking life over yourself:

Uplifting words,

Honest prayers,

Gentle truths,

And sacred time in God's presence.

Each page is an invitation to pause . . . To breathe . . . To listen . . . Here, we choose healing over shame, truth over torment, and faith over fear. Here, we practice holding space for our own hearts the way we do for others—with compassion and grace.

Take a few minutes each day to:

Reflect honestly,

Pray boldly,

Listen deeply, and

Write freely.

Let God meet you in the stillness. Let your own voice echo back strength. You are not broken. You are becoming.

Let each word you write be a step toward peace, victory, and the quiet hope that tomorrow will hold more life than today. Build on your foundation of faith.

Healing is not loud. It is sacred. And it begins here—with you and God. The Lord said:

I will give you the treasures of darkness and the hoards in secret places, that you may know that it is I, the Lord, the God of Israel, who call you by your name. –Isaiah 45:3

With grace and belief in your healing,

Dr. Esmeralda Delgadillo
DPC, LPC, NCC
Licensed Professional Counselor

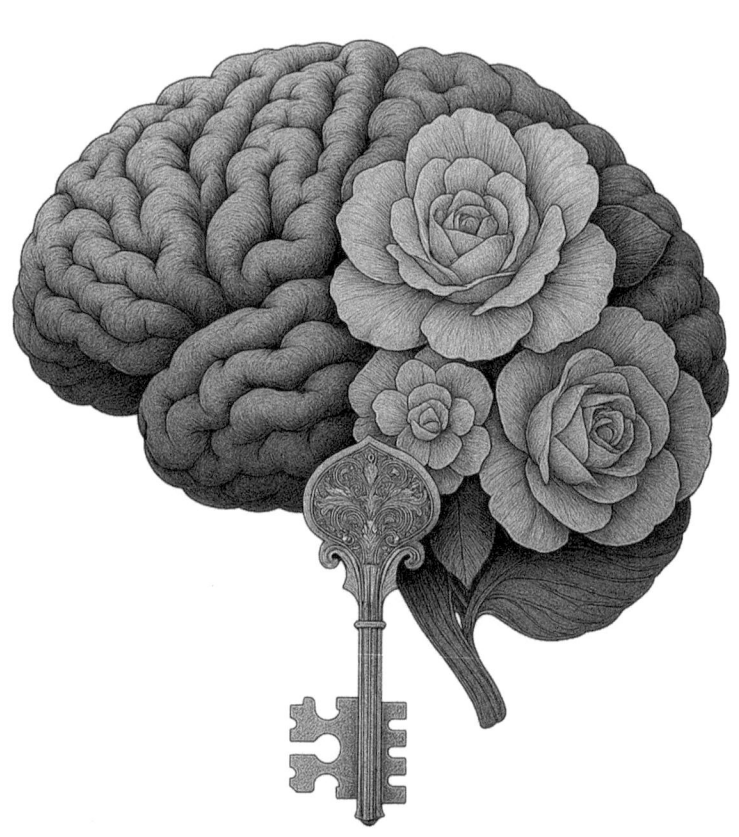

Art Inspiration

The inspiration behind the artwork on this journal comes from a concept I call the Thought Flower. The image of the brain, the flower, and the key symbolizes the unlocking of our thought life.

The mind often carries intrusive and destructive patterns, but when surrendered to God, it becomes fertile soil for renewal. In essence, we can have a beautiful Blooming Mind as we work in the garden of our thoughts. We can release old thought cycles, challenge hidden beliefs, and allow new life-giving memories to take root. A Sacred Bloom emerges through our transformative work. It is a blossom of hope and grace, and a promise which reshapes both the mind and heart.

The Blooming Mind is the unfolding of beauty within the soul. God meets us in the quiet, vulnerable places of our thought life—our garden of life.

This journal a companion for the journey of mindful transformation, unhinging from old patterns, challenging implicit thoughts that keep us bound, and embracing new memories and truths that give life.

In these pages, we will replace destructive thoughts with grace. Fleeting wishes will become lasting hope. What was once heavy will now be light. As we cultivate a Blooming Mind we are reminded that every shift of thought holds the potential for a Sacred Bloom—a blossom of hope, renewal, and promise that will reshape our minds and hearts.

*Within these pages,
I will unlock what
is unspoken.*

*I will find my voice,
discover my peace,
and stay in God's presence.*

A Whisper Within

*And after the earthquake a fire,
but the Lord was not in the fire.
And after the fire the sound of a low whisper.*

I Kings 19:12

AT A GLANCE

TRUTH FOR THE WEEK
What truth do I want to carry with me this week?

MY TOP PRIORITY
What is one small step I can focus on consistently every day?

FOCUS ON SELF-CARE
What can I do to stay connected with God and myself?

MINDFUL HABIT TO BUILD
What habit can I practice to help me grow and meet my goals?

SUPPORT I NEED
What kind of help or space do I need to stay on track?

DATE / / /

Today, I am thankful for . . .

Stresses, feelings, thoughts, beliefs, and behaviors to let go of:

God's truth about my situation is . . .

What I believe about me...

HEAVY THOUGHTS	HELPFUL THOUGHTS

My Prayer

_____
_____
_____
_____
_____
_____

•••••••••••••••••••• SCRIPTURE FOR TODAY ••••••••••••••••••••

_____
_____
_____
_____

DATE / / /

Today, I am thankful for . . .

Stresses, feelings, thoughts, beliefs, and behaviors to let go of:

God's truth about my situation is . . .

What I believe about me . . .

HEAVY THOUGHTS	HELPFUL THOUGHTS

My Prayer

_____
_____
_____
_____
_____
_____

•••••••••••••••••••• SCRIPTURE FOR TODAY ••••••••••••••••••••

_____
_____
_____
_____

DATE / / /

Today, I am thankful for . . .

Stresses, feelings, thoughts, beliefs, and behaviors to let go of:

God's truth about my situation is . . .

What I believe about me . . .

HEAVY THOUGHTS

HELPFUL THOUGHTS

My Prayer

SCRIPTURE FOR TODAY

DATE / / /

Today, I am thankful for . . .

Stresses, feelings, thoughts, beliefs, and behaviors to let go of:

God's truth about my situation is . . .

What I believe about me...

HEAVY THOUGHTS

HELPFUL THOUGHTS

My Prayer

····· SCRIPTURE FOR TODAY ·····

DATE / / /

Today, I am thankful for . . .

Stresses, feelings, thoughts, beliefs, and behaviors to let go of:

God's truth about my situation is . . .

What I believe about me . . .

HEAVY THOUGHTS

HELPFUL THOUGHTS

My Prayer

・・・・・・・・・・・・・・・ SCRIPTURE FOR TODAY ・・・・・・・・・・・・・・・

DATE / / /

Today, I am thankful for . . .

Stresses, feelings, thoughts, beliefs, and behaviors to let go of:

God's truth about my situation is . . .

What I believe about me . . .

HEAVY THOUGHTS

HELPFUL THOUGHTS

My Prayer

SCRIPTURE FOR TODAY

DATE / / /

Today, I am thankful for . . .

Stresses, feelings, thoughts, beliefs, and behaviors to let go of:

God's truth about my situation is . . .

What I believe about me...

HEAVY THOUGHTS

HELPFUL THOUGHTS

My Prayer

······· SCRIPTURE FOR TODAY ·······

Breaking the Silence

*[There is] a time to keep silence,
and a time to speak . . .*

Ecclesiastes 3:7

AT A GLANCE

TRUTH FOR THE WEEK
What truth do I want to carry with me this week?

MY TOP PRIORITY
What is one small step I can focus on consistently every day?

FOCUS ON SELF-CARE
What can I do to stay connected with God and myself?

MINDFUL HABIT TO BUILD
What habit can I practice to help me grow and meet my goals?

SUPPORT I NEED
What kind of help or space do I need to stay on track?

DATE / / /

Today, I am thankful for . . .

Stresses, feelings, thoughts, beliefs, and behaviors to let go of:

God's truth about my situation is . . .

What I believe about me . . .

HEAVY THOUGHTS

HELPFUL THOUGHTS

My Prayer

••••••••••••••••• SCRIPTURE FOR TODAY •••••••••••••••••

DATE / / /

Today, I am thankful for . . .

Stresses, feelings, thoughts, beliefs, and behaviors to let go of:

God's truth about my situation is . . .

What I believe about me . . .

HEAVY THOUGHTS	HELPFUL THOUGHTS

My Prayer

••••••••••••••••••• SCRIPTURE FOR TODAY •••••••••••••••••••

DATE / / /

Today, I am thankful for . . .

Stresses, feelings, thoughts, beliefs, and behaviors to let go of:

God's truth about my situation is . . .

What I believe about me...

HEAVY THOUGHTS

HELPFUL THOUGHTS

My Prayer

_____
_____
_____
_____
_____

•••••••••••••••••• SCRIPTURE FOR TODAY ••••••••••••••••••

_____
_____
_____
_____

DATE / / /

Today, I am thankful for . . .

Stresses, feelings, thoughts, beliefs, and behaviors to let go of:

God's truth about my situation is . . .

What I believe about me . . .

HEAVY THOUGHTS

HELPFUL THOUGHTS

My Prayer

········· SCRIPTURE FOR TODAY ·········

DATE / / /

Today, I am thankful for . . .

Stresses, feelings, thoughts, beliefs, and behaviors to let go of:

God's truth about my situation is . . .

What I believe about me...

HEAVY THOUGHTS	HELPFUL THOUGHTS

My Prayer

_____

_____

_____

_____

_____

·········· SCRIPTURE FOR TODAY ··········

_____

_____

_____

_____

DATE / /

Today, I am thankful for . . .

Stresses, feelings, thoughts, beliefs, and behaviors to let go of:

God's truth about my situation is . . .

What I believe about me . . .

HEAVY THOUGHTS	HELPFUL THOUGHTS

My Prayer

SCRIPTURE FOR TODAY

DATE / / /

Today, I am thankful for . . .

Stresses, feelings, thoughts, beliefs, and behaviors to let go of:

God's truth about my situation is . . .

What I believe about me . . .

HEAVY THOUGHTS

HELPFUL THOUGHTS

My Prayer

······ SCRIPTURE FOR TODAY ······

The Courage of Vulnerability

But he said to me, "My grace is sufficient for you, for my power is made perfect in weakness." Therefore I will boast all the more gladly of my weaknesses, so that the power of Christ may rest upon me.

2 Corinthians 12:9

AT A GLANCE

TRUTH FOR THE WEEK
What truth do I want to carry with me this week?

_____

_____

MY TOP PRIORITY
What is one small step I can focus on consistently every day?

_____

_____

FOCUS ON SELF-CARE
What can I do to stay connected with God and myself?

_____

_____

MINDFUL HABIT TO BUILD
What habit can I practice to help me grow and meet my goals?

_____

_____

SUPPORT I NEED
What kind of help or space do I need to stay on track?

_____

_____

DATE / / /

Today, I am thankful for . . .

Stresses, feelings, thoughts, beliefs, and behaviors to let go of:

God's truth about my situation is . . .

What I believe about me . . .

HEAVY THOUGHTS | **HELPFUL THOUGHTS**

My Prayer

SCRIPTURE FOR TODAY

DATE / / /

Today, I am thankful for . . .

Stresses, feelings, thoughts, beliefs, and behaviors to let go of:

God's truth about my situation is . . .

What I believe about me . . .

HEAVY THOUGHTS

HELPFUL THOUGHTS

My Prayer

SCRIPTURE FOR TODAY

DATE / / /

Today, I am thankful for . . .

Stresses, feelings, thoughts, beliefs, and behaviors to let go of:

God's truth about my situation is . . .

What I believe about me . . .

HEAVY THOUGHTS	HELPFUL THOUGHTS

My Prayer

_____

_____

_____

_____

_____

·········· SCRIPTURE FOR TODAY ··········

....

....

....

....

DATE / / /

Today, I am thankful for . . .

Stresses, feelings, thoughts, beliefs, and behaviors to let go of:

God's truth about my situation is . . .

What I believe about me...

HEAVY THOUGHTS	HELPFUL THOUGHTS

My Prayer

SCRIPTURE FOR TODAY

DATE / / /

Today, I am thankful for . . .

_____

_____

_____

_____

_____

Stresses, feelings, thoughts, beliefs, and behaviors to let go of:

_____

_____

_____

_____

_____

God's truth about my situation is . . .

_____

_____

_____

_____

_____

What I believe about me . . .

HEAVY THOUGHTS

HELPFUL THOUGHTS

My Prayer

SCRIPTURE FOR TODAY

DATE / / /

Today, I am thankful for . . .

Stresses, feelings, thoughts, beliefs, and behaviors to let go of:

God's truth about my situation is . . .

What I believe about me...

HEAVY THOUGHTS

HELPFUL THOUGHTS

My Prayer

············ SCRIPTURE FOR TODAY ············

DATE / / /

Today, I am thankful for . . .

Stresses, feelings, thoughts, beliefs, and behaviors to let go of:

God's truth about my situation is . . .

What I believe about me . . .

HEAVY THOUGHTS

HELPFUL THOUGHTS

My Prayer

············· SCRIPTURE FOR TODAY ·············

Sacred Sound

*Let the words of my mouth and the meditation
of my heart be acceptable in your sight,
O Lord, my rock and my redeemer.*

Psalm 19:14

AT A GLANCE

TRUTH FOR THE WEEK
What truth do I want to carry with me this week?

MY TOP PRIORITY
What is one small step I can focus on consistently every day?

FOCUS ON SELF-CARE
What can I do to stay connected with God and myself?

MINDFUL HABIT TO BUILD
What habit can I practice to help me grow and meet my goals?

SUPPORT I NEED
What kind of help or space do I need to stay on track?

DATE / / /

Today, I am thankful for . . .

Stresses, feelings, thoughts, beliefs, and behaviors to let go of:

God's truth about my situation is . . .

What I believe about me...

HEAVY THOUGHTS

HELPFUL THOUGHTS

My Prayer

••••••••••••••••••• SCRIPTURE FOR TODAY •••••••••••••••••••

DATE / / /

Today, I am thankful for . . .

Stresses, feelings, thoughts, beliefs, and behaviors to let go of:

God's truth about my situation is . . .

What I believe about me...

HEAVY THOUGHTS   **HELPFUL THOUGHTS**

My Prayer

••••••••••••••••• SCRIPTURE FOR TODAY •••••••••••••••••

DATE / / /

Today, I am thankful for . . .

Stresses, feelings, thoughts, beliefs, and behaviors to let go of:

God's truth about my situation is . . .

What I believe about me . . .

HEAVY THOUGHTS

HELPFUL THOUGHTS

My Prayer

SCRIPTURE FOR TODAY

DATE / / /

Today, I am thankful for . . .

Stresses, feelings, thoughts, beliefs, and behaviors to let go of:

God's truth about my situation is . . .

What I believe about me . . .

HEAVY THOUGHTS

HELPFUL THOUGHTS

My Prayer

······· SCRIPTURE FOR TODAY ·······

DATE / / /

Today, I am thankful for . . .

Stresses, feelings, thoughts, beliefs, and behaviors to let go of:

God's truth about my situation is . . .

What I believe about me . . .

HEAVY THOUGHTS

HELPFUL THOUGHTS

My Prayer

••••••••••••••••••••• SCRIPTURE FOR TODAY •••••••••••••••••••••

DATE / / /

Today, I am thankful for . . .

Stresses, feelings, thoughts, beliefs, and behaviors to let go of:

God's truth about my situation is . . .

What I believe about me . . .

HEAVY THOUGHTS

HELPFUL THOUGHTS

My Prayer

••••••••••••••••••• SCRIPTURE FOR TODAY •••••••••••••••••••

DATE / / /

Today, I am thankful for . . .

_____
_____
_____
_____
_____

Stresses, feelings, thoughts, beliefs, and behaviors to let go of:

_____
_____
_____
_____
_____

God's truth about my situation is . . .

_____
_____
_____
_____
_____

What I believe about me...

HEAVY THOUGHTS

HELPFUL THOUGHTS

My Prayer

································· SCRIPTURE FOR TODAY ·································

Keys of the Heart

*He heals the brokenhearted
and binds up their wounds.*

Psalm 147:3

Week Five
AT A GLANCE

TRUTH FOR THE WEEK
What truth do I want to carry with me this week?

_____

_____

MY TOP PRIORITY
What is one small step I can focus on consistently every day?

_____

_____

FOCUS ON SELF-CARE
What can I do to stay connected with God and myself?

_____

_____

MINDFUL HABIT TO BUILD
What habit can I practice to help me grow and meet my goals?

_____

_____

SUPPORT I NEED
What kind of help or space do I need to stay on track?

_____

_____

DATE / / /

Today, I am thankful for . . .

Stresses, feelings, thoughts, beliefs, and behaviors to let go of:

God's truth about my situation is . . .

What I believe about me . . .

HEAVY THOUGHTS

HELPFUL THOUGHTS

My Prayer

SCRIPTURE FOR TODAY

DATE / / /

Today, I am thankful for . . .

Stresses, feelings, thoughts, beliefs, and behaviors to let go of:

God's truth about my situation is . . .

What I believe about me . . .

HEAVY THOUGHTS	HELPFUL THOUGHTS

My Prayer

••••••••••••••••••• SCRIPTURE FOR TODAY ••••••••••••••••••••

DATE / / /

Today, I am thankful for . . .

Stresses, feelings, thoughts, beliefs, and behaviors to let go of:

God's truth about my situation is . . .

What I believe about me . . .

HEAVY THOUGHTS	HELPFUL THOUGHTS

My Prayer

_____
_____
_____
_____
_____

••••••••••••••••••• SCRIPTURE FOR TODAY •••••••••••••••••••

_____
_____
_____
_____

DATE / / /

Today, I am thankful for . . .

Stresses, feelings, thoughts, beliefs, and behaviors to let go of:

God's truth about my situation is . . .

What I believe about me . . .

HEAVY THOUGHTS	HELPFUL THOUGHTS

My Prayer

_____

•••••••••••••••••• SCRIPTURE FOR TODAY ••••••••••••••••••

_____

DATE / / /

Today, I am thankful for . . .

Stresses, feelings, thoughts, beliefs, and behaviors to let go of:

God's truth about my situation is . . .

What I believe about me . . .

HEAVY THOUGHTS

HELPFUL THOUGHTS

My Prayer

SCRIPTURE FOR TODAY

DATE / / /

Today, I am thankful for . . .

Stresses, feelings, thoughts, beliefs, and behaviors to let go of:

God's truth about my situation is . . .

What I believe about me . . .

HEAVY THOUGHTS　　　　　　　**HELPFUL THOUGHTS**

My Prayer

SCRIPTURE FOR TODAY

DATE / / /

Today, I am thankful for . . .

Stresses, feelings, thoughts, beliefs, and behaviors to let go of:

God's truth about my situation is . . .

What I believe about me . . .

HEAVY THOUGHTS

HELPFUL THOUGHTS

My Prayer

SCRIPTURE FOR TODAY

Restored Soul

He restores my soul. He leads me in paths of righteousness for his name's sake.

Psalm 23:3

Week Six
AT A GLANCE

TRUTH FOR THE WEEK
What truth do I want to carry with me this week?

_____
_____

MY TOP PRIORITY
What is one small step I can focus on consistently every day?

_____
_____

FOCUS ON SELF-CARE
What can I do to stay connected with God and myself?

_____
_____

MINDFUL HABIT TO BUILD
What habit can I practice to help me grow and meet my goals?

_____
_____

SUPPORT I NEED
What kind of help or space do I need to stay on track?

_____
_____

DATE / / /

Today, I am thankful for . . .

Stresses, feelings, thoughts, beliefs, and behaviors to let go of:

God's truth about my situation is . . .

What I believe about me . . .

HEAVY THOUGHTS

HELPFUL THOUGHTS

My Prayer

········· SCRIPTURE FOR TODAY ·········

DATE / / /

Today, I am thankful for . . .

___

Stresses, feelings, thoughts, beliefs, and behaviors to let go of:

___

God's truth about my situation is . . .

What I believe about me . . .

HEAVY THOUGHTS	HELPFUL THOUGHTS

My Prayer

_____
_____
_____
_____
_____
_____

•••••••••••••••••••• SCRIPTURE FOR TODAY ••••••••••••••••••••

_____
_____
_____
_____

DATE   /   /   /

Today, I am thankful for . . .

Stresses, feelings, thoughts, beliefs, and behaviors to let go of:

God's truth about my situation is . . .

What I believe about me . . .

HEAVY THOUGHTS | **HELPFUL THOUGHTS**

My Prayer

••••••••••••••• SCRIPTURE FOR TODAY •••••••••••••••

DATE / / /

Today, I am thankful for . . .

Stresses, feelings, thoughts, beliefs, and behaviors to let go of:

God's truth about my situation is . . .

What I believe about me . . .

HEAVY THOUGHTS

HELPFUL THOUGHTS

My Prayer

SCRIPTURE FOR TODAY

DATE / / /

Today, I am thankful for . . .

Stresses, feelings, thoughts, beliefs, and behaviors to let go of:

God's truth about my situation is . . .

What I believe about me...

HEAVY THOUGHTS	HELPFUL THOUGHTS

My Prayer

••••••••••••••••• SCRIPTURE FOR TODAY •••••••••••••••••

DATE / / /

Today, I am thankful for . . .

_____
_____
_____
_____
_____

Stresses, feelings, thoughts, beliefs, and behaviors to let go of:

_____
_____
_____
_____
_____

God's truth about my situation is . . .

_____
_____
_____
_____
_____

What I believe about me . . .

HEAVY THOUGHTS

HELPFUL THOUGHTS

My Prayer

SCRIPTURE FOR TODAY

DATE / / /

Today, I am thankful for . . .

Stresses, feelings, thoughts, beliefs, and behaviors to let go of:

God's truth about my situation is . . .

What I believe about me . . .

HEAVY THOUGHTS

HELPFUL THOUGHTS

My Prayer

••••••••••••••••••••• SCRIPTURE FOR TODAY •••••••••••••••••••••

Holy Tension

"We are afflicted in every way, but not crushed; perplexed, but not driven to despair; persecuted, but snot forsaken; struck down, but not destroyed . . ."

2 Corinthians 4:8-9

AT A GLANCE

TRUTH FOR THE WEEK

What truth do I want to carry with me this week?

MY TOP PRIORITY

What is one small step I can focus on consistently every day?

FOCUS ON SELF-CARE

What can I do to stay connected with God and myself?

MINDFUL HABIT TO BUILD

What habit can I practice to help me grow and meet my goals?

SUPPORT I NEED

What kind of help or space do I need to stay on track?

DATE / / /

Today, I am thankful for . . .

_____
_____
_____
_____
_____

Stresses, feelings, thoughts, beliefs, and behaviors to let go of:

_____
_____
_____
_____
_____

God's truth about my situation is . . .

_____
_____
_____
_____
_____

What I believe about me . . .

HEAVY THOUGHTS

HELPFUL THOUGHTS

My Prayer

········· SCRIPTURE FOR TODAY ·········

DATE / / /

Today, I am thankful for . . .

Stresses, feelings, thoughts, beliefs, and behaviors to let go of:

God's truth about my situation is . . .

What I believe about me . . .

HEAVY THOUGHTS

HELPFUL THOUGHTS

My Prayer

SCRIPTURE FOR TODAY

DATE / / /

Today, I am thankful for . . .

Stresses, feelings, thoughts, beliefs, and behaviors to let go of:

God's truth about my situation is . . .

What I believe about me . . .

HEAVY THOUGHTS	HELPFUL THOUGHTS

My Prayer

_____

_____

_____

_____

_____

•••••••••••••••••••• SCRIPTURE FOR TODAY ••••••••••••••••••••

_____

_____

_____

_____

DATE / / /

Today, I am thankful for . . .

Stresses, feelings, thoughts, beliefs, and behaviors to let go of:

God's truth about my situation is . . .

What I believe about me . . .

HEAVY THOUGHTS

HELPFUL THOUGHTS

My Prayer

········· **SCRIPTURE FOR TODAY** ·········

DATE / / /

Today, I am thankful for . . .

Stresses, feelings, thoughts, beliefs, and behaviors to let go of:

God's truth about my situation is . . .

What I believe about me...

HEAVY THOUGHTS

HELPFUL THOUGHTS

My Prayer

••••••••••••••••••• SCRIPTURE FOR TODAY •••••••••••••••••••

DATE / / /

Today, I am thankful for . . .

Stresses, feelings, thoughts, beliefs, and behaviors to let go of:

God's truth about my situation is . . .

What I believe about me . . .

HEAVY THOUGHTS	HELPFUL THOUGHTS

My Prayer

_____
_____
_____
_____
_____
_____

•••••••••••••••••• SCRIPTURE FOR TODAY ••••••••••••••••••

_____
_____
_____
_____

DATE / / /

Today, I am thankful for . . .

Stresses, feelings, thoughts, beliefs, and behaviors to let go of:

God's truth about my situation is . . .

What I believe about me . . .

HEAVY THOUGHTS

HELPFUL THOUGHTS

My Prayer

SCRIPTURE FOR TODAY

Honor Your Process

"For everything there is a season, and la time for every matter under heaven: a time to be born, and a time to die . . ."

Ecclesiastes 3:1

Week Eight
AT A GLANCE

TRUTH FOR THE WEEK
What truth do I want to carry with me this week?

MY TOP PRIORITY
What is one small step I can focus on consistently every day?

FOCUS ON SELF-CARE
What can I do to stay connected with God and myself?

MINDFUL HABIT TO BUILD
What habit can I practice to help me grow and meet my goals?

SUPPORT I NEED
What kind of help or space do I need to stay on track?

DATE / / /

Today, I am thankful for . . .

Stresses, feelings, thoughts, beliefs, and behaviors to let go of:

God's truth about my situation is . . .

What I believe about me . . .

HEAVY THOUGHTS

HELPFUL THOUGHTS

My Prayer

SCRIPTURE FOR TODAY

DATE / / /

Today, I am thankful for . . .

Stresses, feelings, thoughts, beliefs, and behaviors to let go of:

God's truth about my situation is . . .

What I believe about me . . .

HEAVY THOUGHTS

HELPFUL THOUGHTS

My Prayer

········· SCRIPTURE FOR TODAY ·········

DATE / / /

Today, I am thankful for . . .

Stresses, feelings, thoughts, beliefs, and behaviors to let go of:

God's truth about my situation is . . .

What I believe about me . . .

HEAVY THOUGHTS	HELPFUL THOUGHTS

My Prayer

••••••••••••••••••• SCRIPTURE FOR TODAY •••••••••••••••••••

DATE / / /

Today, I am thankful for . . .

Stresses, feelings, thoughts, beliefs, and behaviors to let go of:

God's truth about my situation is . . .

What I believe about me . . .

HEAVY THOUGHTS	HELPFUL THOUGHTS

My Prayer

•••••••••••••••••••••• SCRIPTURE FOR TODAY ••••••••••••••••••••••

DATE / / /

Today, I am thankful for . . .

___

___

___

___

___

Stresses, feelings, thoughts, beliefs, and behaviors to let go of:

___

___

___

___

___

God's truth about my situation is . . .

___

___

___

___

___

What I believe about me . . .

HEAVY THOUGHTS

HELPFUL THOUGHTS

My Prayer

······· SCRIPTURE FOR TODAY ·······

DATE / / /

Today, I am thankful for . . .

Stresses, feelings, thoughts, beliefs, and behaviors to let go of:

God's truth about my situation is . . .

What I believe about me . . .

HEAVY THOUGHTS	HELPFUL THOUGHTS

My Prayer

_____

_____

_____

_____

_____

······· SCRIPTURE FOR TODAY ·······

_____

_____

_____

_____

DATE / / /

Today, I am thankful for . . .

Stresses, feelings, thoughts, beliefs, and behaviors to let go of:

God's truth about my situation is . . .

What I believe about me . . .

HEAVY THOUGHTS	HELPFUL THOUGHTS

My Prayer

_____
_____
_____
_____
_____

••••••••••••••••• SCRIPTURE FOR TODAY •••••••••••••••••

_____
_____
_____
_____

Write Your Healing

"Let not steadfast love and faithfulness forsake you; bind them around your neck; write them on the tablet of your heart."

Proverbs 3:3

AT A GLANCE

TRUTH FOR THE WEEK
What truth do I want to carry with me this week?

MY TOP PRIORITY
What is one small step I can focus on consistently every day?

FOCUS ON SELF-CARE
What can I do to stay connected with God and myself?

MINDFUL HABIT TO BUILD
What habit can I practice to help me grow and meet my goals?

SUPPORT I NEED
What kind of help or space do I need to stay on track?

DATE / / /

Today, I am thankful for . . .

Stresses, feelings, thoughts, beliefs, and behaviors to let go of:

God's truth about my situation is . . .

What I believe about me . . .

HEAVY THOUGHTS

HELPFUL THOUGHTS

My Prayer

· · · · · · · · · · · · · · · SCRIPTURE FOR TODAY · · · · · · · · · · · · · · ·

DATE / / /

Today, I am thankful for . . .

Stresses, feelings, thoughts, beliefs, and behaviors to let go of:

God's truth about my situation is . . .

What I believe about me . . .

HEAVY THOUGHTS

HELPFUL THOUGHTS

My Prayer

SCRIPTURE FOR TODAY

DATE / / /

Today, I am thankful for . . .

Stresses, feelings, thoughts, beliefs, and behaviors to let go of:

God's truth about my situation is . . .

What I believe about me . . .

HEAVY THOUGHTS

HELPFUL THOUGHTS

My Prayer

••••••••••••••••• SCRIPTURE FOR TODAY ••••••••••••••••••

DATE / / /

Today, I am thankful for . . .

Stresses, feelings, thoughts, beliefs, and behaviors to let go of:

God's truth about my situation is . . .

What I believe about me . . .

HEAVY THOUGHTS	HELPFUL THOUGHTS

My Prayer

••••••••••••••••••• SCRIPTURE FOR TODAY •••••••••••••••••••

DATE / / /

Today, I am thankful for . . .

Stresses, feelings, thoughts, beliefs, and behaviors to let go of:

God's truth about my situation is . . .

What I believe about me...

HEAVY THOUGHTS	HELPFUL THOUGHTS

My Prayer

••••••••••••••••••••• SCRIPTURE FOR TODAY •••••••••••••••••••••

DATE / / /

Today, I am thankful for . . .

Stresses, feelings, thoughts, beliefs, and behaviors to let go of:

God's truth about my situation is . . .

What I believe about me . . .

HEAVY THOUGHTS

HELPFUL THOUGHTS

My Prayer

SCRIPTURE FOR TODAY

DATE / / /

Today, I am thankful for . . .

Stresses, feelings, thoughts, beliefs, and behaviors to let go of:

God's truth about my situation is . . .

What I believe about me . . .

HEAVY THOUGHTS

HELPFUL THOUGHTS

My Prayer

SCRIPTURE FOR TODAY

Unveiling Truth

"You will know the truth,
and the truth will set you free."

John 8:32

AT A GLANCE

TRUTH FOR THE WEEK
What truth do I want to carry with me this week?

MY TOP PRIORITY
What is one small step I can focus on consistently every day?

FOCUS ON SELF-CARE
What can I do to stay connected with God and myself?

MINDFUL HABIT TO BUILD
What habit can I practice to help me grow and meet my goals?

SUPPORT I NEED
What kind of help or space do I need to stay on track?

DATE / / /

Today, I am thankful for . . .

Stresses, feelings, thoughts, beliefs, and behaviors to let go of:

God's truth about my situation is . . .

What I believe about me . . .

HEAVY THOUGHTS

HELPFUL THOUGHTS

My Prayer

····· SCRIPTURE FOR TODAY ·····

DATE / / /

Today, I am thankful for . . .

Stresses, feelings, thoughts, beliefs, and behaviors to let go of:

God's truth about my situation is . . .

What I believe about me...

HEAVY THOUGHTS

HELPFUL THOUGHTS

My Prayer

······ SCRIPTURE FOR TODAY ······

DATE / / /

Today, I am thankful for . . .

___

Stresses, feelings, thoughts, beliefs, and behaviors to let go of:

___

God's truth about my situation is . . .

___

What I believe about me . . .

HEAVY THOUGHTS	HELPFUL THOUGHTS

My Prayer

••••••••••••••••• SCRIPTURE FOR TODAY •••••••••••••••••

DATE / / /

Today, I am thankful for . . .

Stresses, feelings, thoughts, beliefs, and behaviors to let go of:

God's truth about my situation is . . .

What I believe about me . . .

HEAVY THOUGHTS

HELPFUL THOUGHTS

My Prayer

• • • • • • • • • • • • • • • SCRIPTURE FOR TODAY • • • • • • • • • • • • • • •

DATE / / /

Today, I am thankful for . . .

Stresses, feelings, thoughts, beliefs, and behaviors to let go of:

God's truth about my situation is . . .

What I believe about me . . .

HEAVY THOUGHTS | **HELPFUL THOUGHTS**

My Prayer

········· SCRIPTURE FOR TODAY ·········

DATE / / /

Today, I am thankful for . . .

_____

_____

_____

_____

Stresses, feelings, thoughts, beliefs, and behaviors to let go of:

_____

_____

_____

_____

God's truth about my situation is . . .

_____

_____

_____

_____

What I believe about me . . .

HEAVY THOUGHTS

HELPFUL THOUGHTS

My Prayer

SCRIPTURE FOR TODAY

DATE / / /

Today, I am thankful for . . .

Stresses, feelings, thoughts, beliefs, and behaviors to let go of:

God's truth about my situation is . . .

What I believe about me . . .

HEAVY THOUGHTS

HELPFUL THOUGHTS

My Prayer

······· SCRIPTURE FOR TODAY ·······

Within these pages,
I have unlocked what
has been unspoken.

I have found my voice,
discovered my peace,
and stayed in God's presence.

www.ingramcontent.com/pod-product-compliance
Lightning Source LLC
Chambersburg PA
CBHW061808070526
44586CB00024B/2760